Dedication

To my beloved grandmother, whose wisdom
and love have shaped my life,

To my sister, my confidante and greatest
supporter,

And to my parents, whose unwavering belief
in me has been my guiding light.

This book is for you, with all my love and
gratitude.

Acknowledgment

I want to extend my heartfelt gratitude to everyone who has supported me on this journey. To my family, thank you for your love, even when the road has been rocky. Your presence has shaped my understanding of resilience and hope.

To my grandmother, whose wisdom and strength have been a guiding light in my life. Your stories inspire me every day. To my sister, my constant companion and cheerleader, thank you for always being there to listen and uplift me.

Finally, to anyone who has shared their own experiences with mental health—your bravery has inspired me to find my voice and share my truth. This book is as much yours as it is mine.
With gratitude,

Preface

Welcome to my collection of poetry, a journey through the intricate landscape of my thoughts and emotions. This book is a reflection of my experiences with mental health, a subject that often feels heavy yet is so vital to understanding who I am.

Throughout my life, I've navigated the complexities of family dynamics and the impact of relatives whose words and actions have left deep marks on my heart. In these pages, you'll find verses that explore the struggles of feeling misunderstood, the weight of silence when no one speaks up, and the courage it takes to find my voice.

Writing has been my solace—a way to express what often felt too difficult to share. These poems are raw and honest, capturing moments of pain, resilience, and ultimately, hope. I hope they resonate with you and remind you that you are not alone in your journey.

Thank you for joining me in this exploration of love, loss, and healing. May these words offer comfort and connection and perhaps inspire you to reflect on your own experiences.
With love,

A NEW LIGHT

The pain may come, the scars may stay,
but you can find a brighter way.
with every tear and every fall,
you rise again; you stand tall.

You are more than hurt and strife
There's hope and love in your Life.

HEART AND MIND

The heart, a hollow muscle, they say,
Pumps blood through our veins, day after day.
Yet when I'm hurt, it aches so deep,
Clutching my chest as I silently weep.
Why does it feel like logic should reign?
Why does it hurt with this heavy pain?
It's all in my brain, yet here it resides,
A wild little thing that I try to hide.
Trapped in a cage, this heart beats loud,
Longing for freedom, yet lost in the crowd.
I'm tired of wrestling with feelings so raw,
Tired of fighting this internal war.
I've given up trying to understand,

This complex dance, this shaky ground.
But maybe it's okay to let it all be,
To feel every ache, to just let me see.

I'M A PARADOX

"I'm a paradox.

I want to be happy, but I think of things that make me sad.

I'm lazy, yet I'm ambitious.

I don't like myself, but I also love who I am.

I say I don't really care, but I really do.

I crave attention but reject it when it comes my way.

If I can't figure myself out, there is NO way anyone else has."

"YOU ARE THE KIND OF MYSTERY I
wouldn't mind spending the rest of my life
trying to figure it out."
We'll get through this life together. My pretty
wonderful "OLD SOUL."

SUNFLOWERS OVER ROSES

Most give roses, bright and fair,
But I wonder, do they really care?
Roses are pretty, but they've got thorns,
A beauty that hides where hurt can be born.
Instead, let's choose sunflowers, bold and bright,
They reach for the sun, chasing the light.
Tell her to be like those flowers that grow,
Facing the dark with the strength to show.

She doesn't need protection from fear,
Just confidence to hold her dear.
So when you pick a flower to share,
Choose sunflowers—a gift that's rare.

A Light in the Dark

In my lowest moments, when shadows fell,
You were my anchor, my guiding spell.
With gentle words and a knowing smile,
You stayed by my side through every trial.
Your hands, so warm, held my aching heart,
In silence, you listened—a true work of art.
You shared your stories, your laughter, your grace,
Reminding me of love in this difficult place.
Through tears and struggles, you showed me the way,
With you by my side, I found hope each day.
A soft, steady light in my darkest hour,

Grandma, you're my strength, my sweetest power.
Now I look back, and I see so clear,
How your love lifted me, year after year.
Forever, I cherish the bond that we share,
Thank you, dear Grandma, for always being there.

Missing Those Rides

I think of the days when you'd take me for a
spin,
Riding on the bike, feeling the thrill within.
You'd laugh as I'd squeal, arms wrapped tight,
Those carefree moments, pure joy and light.
Now you're so busy, caught in the grind,
Chasing deadlines, leaving those days behind.
I miss our adventures, just you and me,
The wind in my hair, feeling so free.
As a grown woman, I cherish those times,
The laughter, the love, the sweet simple
rhymes.
Though life pulls you far, those memories stay,
Wishing for bike rides to come back my way.

MOM, The Braveheart

In moments of trouble, when fear took its
hold,
You stood up for us, steady and bold.
When no one else could, you faced the
unknown,
With courage, that showed we were never
alone.
You carried the weight with strength in your
eyes,
Calming our worries, dispelling the cries.

Through storms and uncertainty, you led the
way,
A brave heart in darkness, turning night into
day.
Your love was a shield, your spirit so bright,
In the hardest of times, you were our light.
So here's to you, Mom, our fearless guide,
A warrior at heart, with love as your pride.

Silence in the Room

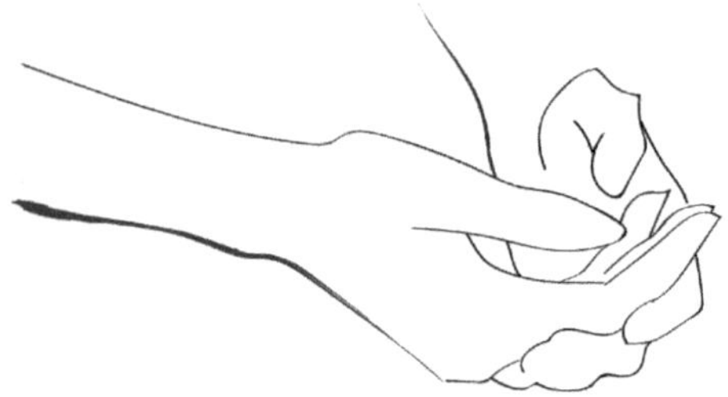

In the quiet office, I sit in my chair,
Words feel so heavy, too hard to share.
The clock ticks softly, my thoughts start to
race,
I search for the courage, but it hides without
trace.
Across from me, a warm, knowing gaze,
A safe space created, but I'm lost in a maze.
My heart beats loudly, my mind feels so still,
I want to speak freely but can't find the will.
Memories swirl like leaves in the breeze,
Each one a struggle, each one a tease.
I swallow the feelings, the fears that I hide,
Wanting connection but feeling denied.
But here in this silence, I know it's okay,
To take my time, to feel my own way.

One breath at a time, I'll find my own voice,
In this quiet moment, I'll make my own
choice.

Hungry But Unable

My stomach growls softly, I feel the ache,
But here I sit frozen, unable to take.
Food looks so tempting, so warm and so near,
Yet something inside me just holds back the
fear.
I crave for the comfort, the taste of the meal,
But each time I try, I can't seem to feel.
Caught in a struggle, my heart feels so tight,
Hungry for something but not ready to bite.
I long for a moment to break through this
wall,
To find the courage to answer the call.
One step at a time, I'll learn to embrace,
The joy of the food, the warmth in this space.

Doing What I Love

I wake with a spark, ready to create,
Chasing my dreams, ignoring the hate.
Not everyone gets it; they don't understand,
But I'll keep on moving, I'll take my own
stand.
With every brush stroke or word that I write,
I find my own joy, and it feels so right.
Though doubts may linger, I won't lose my
way,
I'll do what I love, come what may.
In the things that I cherish, I find my true
place,
Following my passion, I embrace the chase.
So here's to my journey, no matter the cost,
In doing what I love, I'll never be lost.

Living with Bipolar

Some days I'm up, feeling on top,
Full of energy, I never want to stop.
But then it can shift, the clouds rolling in,
Sudden and heavy, where do I begin?
Thoughts race like lightning, then slow down
to a crawl,
A whirlwind of feelings, I'm trying to stand
tall.
Joy turns to sadness, laughter fades away,
A battle inside me, come what may.
I ride the high waves, then sink in the deep,
Learning to navigate this journey I keep.
But through all the changes, I find my own
way,
Embracing the rhythms, day by day.

I am not just my highs or my lows,
I'm a mix of emotions, and that's how it goes.
With each twist and turn, I learn to be free,
Finding my strength in just being me.

Getting Out of Bed

The morning light creeps through my door,
But the weight of my sadness makes me want
to ignore.
I lie here in silence, wrapped up in dread,
Wishing for the courage to leave my warm
bed.
Each day feels heavy, too hard to face,
The world feels so distant, a cold, empty
space.
I want to get up to feel the sun's glow,

But the struggle inside makes it hard to let go.
Yet deep down, I know there's a spark that
can grow,
A small piece of hope I'm learning to show.
So today I'll try, just one step ahead,
Finding my strength to rise from my bed.

Happy on My Own

I wake with the sun, ready to start,
Finding my joy; it's a gift from the heart.
With quiet moments and space to be free,
I learn to embrace just being me.
I fill my day with things that I love,
A book, a warm drink, the sky up above.
No need for the noise or a crowd all around,
In my own company, true peace can be found.
I dance in my room, I laugh with the breeze,
Finding my happiness with simple ease.
I'm learning to shine; no need to pretend,
Happy on my own, my own best friend.

Silent Pain

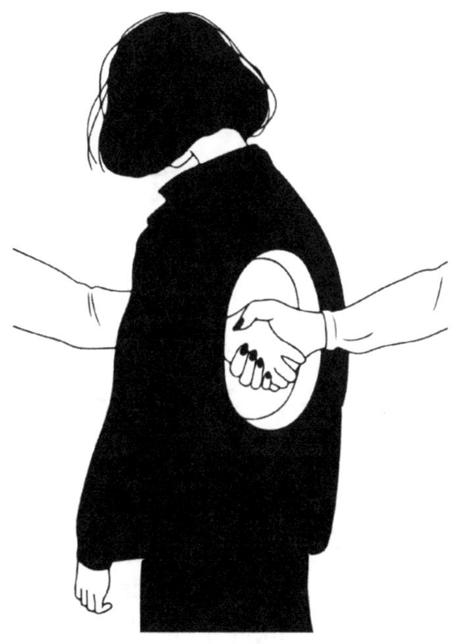

In shadows I linger, my spirit worn thin,
A battle inside me, where do I begin?
Family ties tangled in secrets and lies,
Everyone knows, but they turn blind eyes.
Trust has been shattered, love feels like dust,
I carry this weight, but at what cost?
Each whispered moment, my pain goes
unseen,
Haunted by memories of what could have
been.

He walks free, while I bear the scars,
A silent survivor, reaching for stars.
But deep in my heart, a fire still glows,
Strength is a seed that only I know.
So here is my journey, though heavy the load,
I'll rise from the ashes; I'll find my own road.
With courage unyielding, I'll break through the night,
A warrior at heart, ready to fight.

Torn by Betrayal

In the shadows, they whisper, with smiles that deceive,
Relatives who want us to break and not believe.
They sow seeds of doubt, trying to pull us apart,
But we stand together, united at heart.
Their words may sting, but we'll rise above,
Family is stronger when built on true love.
We'll hold each other through the storm and the strife,
Together we'll flourish, with hope in our life.

Let them keep talking; let them play their
game,
We know who we are; we won't feel their
shame.
In our bond, we find strength; in trust, we'll
survive,
Against all their efforts, our family's alive.

Words That Echo

I still remember what you said,
Your words never leave; they circle my head.
"You're not welcome here," you made it so
clear,
But deep down, I know it's my home, my
sphere.
Just a relative, greedy, with darkness inside,
Your abusive mindset, you wear like a pride.
I listened to you but left for my peace,
Not because of you, but for love to increase.
My family stayed silent; your grip was so
tight,
Manipulating them well, you dimmed the
light.

But I'll reclaim my voice; I'll stand on my
own,
For my home is my heart, and love has been
sown.
Your words may have stung, but they won't
hold me down,
I'll rise from the ashes; I'll wear my own
crown.
For I know who I am, and I won't turn away,
In the strength of my truth, I'll find my own
way.

Silent Shadows

In the quiet corners, the whispers remain,
A relative roams free, carrying shame.
Abuser in shadows, his actions well known,
Yet everyone stays silent, the truth
overthrown.
He walks with a smirk, while we feel the
weight,
The hurt he has caused, the anger, the fate.
Guilt lingers heavy, like a dark, heavy shroud,

But no one will speak; no one is loud.
They turn their heads, pretending it's fine,
While pain festers deep, like an unbroken
line.
The fear holds them back, keeps them in
place,
As he roams through the world, without a
trace of grace.
But deep down inside, we know what is right,
And though we stay quiet, we carry the fight.
One day the truth will rise, break free from
the night,
For love will find courage, and darkness will
light.

Betrayed by Blood

You thought it was easy, your choices so sly,
But family should stand, not just watch from
the side.
You broke my father's trust, and it cut us all
deep,
As brothers and sisters turned quiet, not
steep.
You chose to betray, leaving pain in your
wake,
Trading love for your secrets, for your own
selfish sake.

Now the bonds are all frayed, the hurt still
remains,
A family divided, carrying chains.
Remember the price for the trust that you
stole,
When loyalty fades, it can take such a toll.
Though the pain lingers on, we'll find our
own way,
For love will endure, and we'll be okay.

Sorry for Not Being

I'm sorry, Mom, for not being what you planned,
For the times I've let you down, I hope you understand.
I know you wanted a daughter so bright,
But sometimes I struggle, lost in the night.
I'm trying my best to find my own way,
Thank you for your love, day after day.
I may not be perfect, but I'm still here,
Working to grow, with you always near.

The Rebel I Am

I'm the rebel daughter my family won't see,
Living my truth, just being me.
With fire in my heart and dreams that run
wild,
I break all the rules, an unplanned child.
You wanted me quiet, on a safe, simple path,
But I chase my own dreams, embracing the
wrath.
I'm loud and I'm proud, with a spirit so free,

Not fitting the mold that you wanted for me.
Though you may not approve of the choices I make,
I'm finding my voice, and I won't hesitate.
So here I stand strong, ready to shine,
A rebel, a dreamer, this life is mine.

Single by Choice

I walk my own path, and I'm happy this way,
No need for a partner to brighten my day.
With dreams in my heart and a spark in my soul,
I'm finding my joy; I'm feeling quite whole.
I cherish my freedom, the space to explore,
With time for myself, I can open new doors.
I laugh and I dance; I travel and roam,
Creating my story, I've made it my home.
No pressure to fit into someone else's plan,
I'm thriving alone, and I truly can.
With every new day, I embrace who I am,
Single by choice, I'm proud to take a stand.

So here's to my journey, my life full of light,
I'm loving the moments; my future is bright.
With strength in my heart, I'll follow my
voice,
Living my truth, I rejoice in my choice.

Two Halves

Part of me will always be,
A shadow cast, a memory.
But the other part, set free and whole,
Is happier than it's ever been before.

The Spark

It started as a flicker,
A midnight spark, a whispered dare.
Just one small thought, unseen by most,
Yet now it's real, and everywhere.
People gather, lend their skills,
Shaping dreams with an iron will.
Each step forward, side by side,
Breathing life into that midnight light.
They're here for something bigger still—
An idea, a purpose, a shared thrill.
And through their hands, I watch it grow,
More than I imagined, more than I'd know.

Restless Comfort

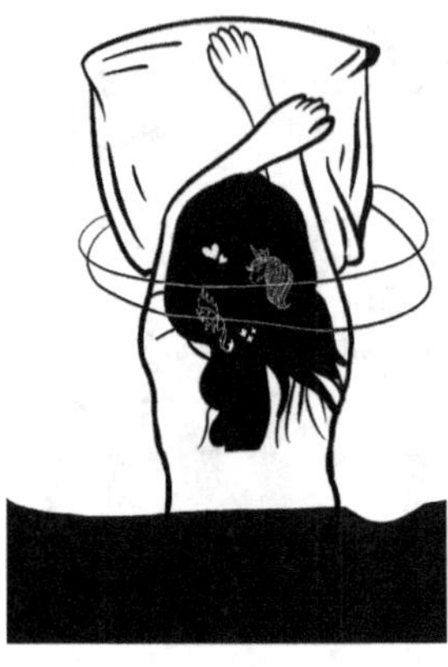

I need comfort, but hate the still,
Craving peace, yet chasing thrill.
Held by warmth, but bound by fire—
A restless heart, a wild desire.

Melodies of Healing

In darkened days, their voices came,
A song, a light, a steady flame.
Through every beat and lyric spun,
I found my strength; my battles won.

Better On Paper

Samantha Reed

BookLeaf
Publishing